Cabin Fever

Ruby F. Nazaruk

Books by Ruby F. Nazaruk

Story Collections

Words In All Their Splendor
A String Called Love
A Journey of People & Ourselves
Do You Have a Pen?
A Trail of What if's & Love
The Author's Mind
Bedtime Stories for Children
Leaves & their Whispers
Soul's Intertwined
The Bizarre & Strange Story Collection
The Heart of Paradise
Unspoken: A Collection of Words Left Unsaid
Waves & Their Secrets

Ruby's Faith Collection

God Instances
A Journey with Our Lady
God's Call

Ruby's Learning Collection

Living Life with Dyslexia

Cabin Fever

RUBY F. NAZARUK

Copyright © 2026 Ruby F. Nazaruk

All rights reserved.

ISBN: 978-1-998666-08-9

DEDICATION

I dedicate this book to my grandfather,
Charles Rypien.

CONTENTS

ACKNOWLEDGMENTS

I really enjoyed creating this story collection. A big thank you to all those who continue to support and encourage me. For my family and friends.

1 WEAPONS

She was determined to write.
As though she was running out of time,
as if driven by some invisible force,
urging her onward,
pushing her breath into ink,
Her silence into sound.
Urging her onward
to speak out in her way—
with her pen and her page,
her weapons in a war
She didn't ask for wages around her.
Yet there she found herself,
in the center of it all,
caught between truth and noise,
between the weight of voices
And the clarity of her own.
Clinging to hope,
To all she knows to be true,
She carved each word like a lifeline,
like a lantern against the dark,
determined that her story
would not be silenced,
That her voice would rise
Even when the world tried to drown it.

2 TRAVELERS

She befriended a boy.
Who was oceans away,
Yet he filled the space of silence.
Within the night.
Sun upon the girl's face,
the quiet, soothing sounds of nature
whispering songs of harmony,
Woven into the breath of wind.
A realm hidden away,
A place one seeks.
A lone traveler with a birch staff,
a merry band of wanderers
met upon gravel roads—
adventure seekers, dreamers,
Those who watched the setting sun
and the colors dancing
Through the birch forest.
Beaver dams of wood and mud,
thistles rising, wild grass swaying,
a creek nestled in its own little home—
a place untouched,

Unmanned by society,
By city folk.
The silence of the world.
The brief rustle of grass
in the morning wind,
a loon calling in the distance,
the ripping rush of water
within the creek,
the tree line reflected back—
a world of its own,
tucked away behind fields
And rows of trees.
A place of nature.
A place of wonder.

3 WRITERS OF OLD

I wonder about the past writers,
the storytellers of old,
Whose voices carried through the night
Around the campfire and torchlight.
The hearth and candles
filled up the room—
the smell of wax,
the warmth radiating from them,
the flickering and dancing of flames
casting shadows like spirits
upon the walls,
And breathing life into every tale.
They told of heroes,
of journeys through forests and seas,
of love and loss,
of beasts and gods,
Their words are a bridge between the
ordinary.
And the marvelous.
The darkness would settle in,
Yet it was never empty—
It was a stage for imagination,
a canvas for wonder,
A quiet space where stories could grow

And bloom.
I wonder what it was like
to live entirely within such nights,
before electricity,
before the hum of screens,
Before the endless pull of social media.
To write then
was to step closer to the pulse of the world,
to feel its silence,
to hear the whispers of wind and fire,
to let the mind wander
And the heart remembers
The mysteries hidden in shadow.
And even now,
Though the lights are bright,
Though distraction surrounds,
The wonder remains waiting—
As it always has—
Ready for those who pause,
who listen,
Who let the stories find them?

4 LONE TRAVELER

There was a lone traveler.
They traversed the lands.
As far as the eye could see—
walls of trees rising tall,
open spaces stretching wide,
creeks winding their silver ribbons,
and still bodies of water
Holding the sky within them.
The sun was setting,
slipping lower,
Painting the earth in firelight.
The evening glow was enchanted,
its warmth lingering,
Its breath is soft as a sigh.
Orange hues enchanted birch trees,
their pale trunks catching the light,
as if the forest itself
Had caught flame.
Lone Traveler in the Woods.
Lone traveler,
walking the gravel roads,
each stone a rhythm beneath their step,
ember's glow on birch trees
Guiding them forward.

And in memory,
Home was never far:
the promise of Donair's,
Gummies traded between fingers,
sticky with laughter,
country tunes on the radio
Humming like a heartbeat.
Siblings by their side,
Family gathered close—
The journey was never lonely,
For even when the road stretched
endlessly,
the thought of home
Pulled them onward.
Lone traveler,
still wandering,
still searching,
Yet always bound
to the ember glow,
to the gravel road,
To the song that calls them
Homeward bound.

5 SLEEPLESS

The nights of sleeplessness
Brought different experiences.
Some nights, depression.
Others, creative,
And spent with a pen in hand.
Well, nights like these
could lead to thoughts
Tumbling upon the pages.
Some of the best inspiration
can come in the dead of night—
Perhaps the rants and ravings
of a deranged author,
Or one who had become drunk
on a lack of sleep,
Seeking some kind of restitution.
Yet, somewhere in all of that,
stories emerge—
Stories that turn into something more
than just a mad weaving of words,
more than the restless scribblings
of a mad woman
trying to tell,
And tune herself out,
And lull herself into sleep.

OH—

what stories will she think of next?

6 FOGGY

It was clouded over and foggy,
The world around is wrapped in gray.
Dreary skies lingered,
As though fall had fully settled in—
colors melting together,
summer fading quietly into memory,
And autumn is reaching its golden pinnacle.
The mornings grew crisp,
The nights are colder still,
A whisper of winter waits just beyond the
horizon.
And yet, there was beauty in it all—
in every fleeting moment,
in every breath of chilled air,
In every leaf turned gold and crimson.
A warm cup of tea in hand felt like a hug,
a reminder to linger, to savor,
To embrace what the season offers.
Fall is here to stay,
At least until winter comes
To claim the earth in its quiet embrace.

7 SEASONS

Time moves quickly,
days slipping into weeks,
Seasons shift in quiet rhythm.
And yet—how lovely it is to pause,
To see it all with one's own eyes:
the textures, the colors, the layers,
As though the world itself were a painting.
Sometimes a picture may hold a
thousand words,
But often there are no words.
To truly capture such beauty.
The scenic roads, the winding paths—
Familiar, yet never the same.
Each time they draw you in,
Each time they spark joy and quiet wonder.
Fall unfolds in its blanket of warmth,
leaves changing, tumbling,
welcoming the heart into a season of color
And inspiration.

8 AMONGST THE TREES

Something I love about fall is the way certain clusters of trees seem to arrange themselves, layered and staggered as though an artist carefully placed each one. The colors blend together so naturally, creating a living canvas of reds, golds, and deep amber tones that ripple through the branches.

They harmonize as if they were meant to be side by side, each shade complementing the other, drawing you in like brushstrokes across a masterpiece.

Oh, how vibrant and breathtaking it can be—this natural art, this gift of God's creation.

To stand before it is to feel both small and filled with wonder, to realize that beauty doesn't always need to be crafted by human hands.

How lovely it is to walk among those trees, to breathe in the crisp air, and to let the tapestry of colors settle upon the heart like a song of the season.

9 TIMES PASSAGE

There is a passage of time.
Some moments we notice—
the subtle changes of aging,
The ways we grow and shift as we move
through life.
Other parts simply slip by,
Vanishing into the mist of days we barely
pay attention to.
We chase the seasons,
or the passing of those around us,
And in the rush, we become distracted.
Connections fade.
We lose touch.
And everyone knows it.
So much time—so many moments—
Slip quietly away,
Leaving only memory in their wake.

10 VANISHED SUMMER

Summer seemed to vanish, slipping
quietly through our fingers.
I don't know where it went—
The days flew by so quickly.
Here we are, nearing the end of August,
And already the first hints of fall are in the
air.
The warmth is fading,
rainy days creeping in,
And soon winter will follow.
Yet there is a sweetness in thinking
ahead,
dreaming of the first Christmas together as
a married couple,
The first holiday we will share,
Creating new memories side by side.
Oh, how lovely it is to look forward to the
future,
To wonder at all it may bring,
To feel the quiet excitement of what lies
ahead.

11 POPLAR TREES

Poplar trees rise tall and proud,
Lining the narrow stretch of dirt road that seems to go on forever.
The path winds through tight turns,
Its deep yellow signs mark corners like small sentinels.
Oh, how vast this place can feel,
As though the world has opened just for you.
It is enchanting, alive with secrets.
lurking behind every legendary tree,
Whispering stories only the wind can carry.
Each step along the road invites discovery,
A quiet promise of wonder hidden just out of sight.

12 WRITING BUG

The writing bug has arrived,
For such an itch, I haven't scratched.
As much as I would have liked in the past.
Life grows busy,
And sometimes words must wait in the
wings,
Yet the heart still lives and breathes
through the written word.
It is hard to go too long without a pen in
hand.
So here the writer sits,
taking a quiet breath,
Before letting the river of words flow.
The thoughts splash onto the page like
salmon,
swimming upstream,
determined to reach the other side—
A place where so much is held within.
What will they say,
these words,
When they land upon the page,
When they are finally seen, read, and felt?

13 EVENING COMES

Evening comes faster now,
Darkness is settling in sooner with each
passing day.
Birds take to the sky in their familiar V-
shaped formations,
A quiet signal of seasons shifting.
The crops slowly sway in the fields,
Some are being harvested, others are still
standing tall.
Fall is just around the corner,
As August slips away and summer quietly
fades.
Colors streak across the evening sky,
the sun sinking lower,
Hinting at the cooler days to come.
Leaves are already beginning to change,
Painting the world in golds, reds, and
amber.
Soon fall will give way to winter,
And the long, quiet months will unfold.
Time moves ever onward,
And we move with it,
Witnessing the steady, gentle rhythm of the
seasons.

14 THE JOURNEY

There was that winding road—
That road that eventually would lead me home.
Winding paths, gravel stretches,
Twisting and turning, yet always guiding me forward.
I travel it slowly,
relishing each curve, each sunlit bend,
Knowing that it is the path that leads me to you—
Home to you, my love.
Oh, how lovely it is to journey down such a road,
to take the scenic route,
To let the unexpected unfold along the way.
Sometimes the path is long,
Sometimes it's the journey itself that
matters more than the destination.
And yet,
At the end, there is a place to rest,
to arrive, to experience, to embrace—
And it is beautiful in every step.

15 WAITING

It was within the quiet moments of
waiting.
That it came in whispers—
soft, steady, almost like a breeze
through a half-opened window,
A story that needed to be told,
One that pressed against the edges of
silence,
Asking to be heard.
How one might lose hope,
Yet not despair,
For it was far from over.
The thread was not cut,
the light not extinguished,
Only dimmed in the fog of uncertainty.
It was just in the middle of the chapter of
transition,
a turning page not yet written,
An unfolding that would bring change,
a change carried in both ache and promise,
And with it, resolve—
The kind that shapes itself in stillness,
waiting for the moment to step forward
Into what comes next.

16 FLIPPING PAGES

She watched the pages being flipped
through in her hands.
For a moment, she wondered—was it time?
Time to speak, not with a voice,
But with words stretched across the page.
She had been silent for so long,
Holding her tongue, abiding her own time.
All the words left unsaid had filled the
pages,
And now, here they were, printed for all to
see.
It was time to emerge from the ashes,
To rise from all that had tried to bring her
down,
From those who had tried to snuff out her
light and joy
Because they themselves had lost it.
They had sought to destroy what they
could not have,
To crush what was good and bright,
For it was easier to destroy
Than to face the monsters they had
become.
But she could not be broken.

Her words endured.
Her light persisted.
Her voice, long held in silence, finally spoke,
And in that speaking, she was free.

17 COVERED IN FOG

It was a crisp September morning,
The kind where breath hangs heavy in the air,
and the world—
the whole world—
It was coated in fog.
The fog ate everything,
swallowed it whole,
So thick you couldn't see the road ahead,
So near it wrapped itself around you,
So far, it erased the horizon.
It consumed,
It cloaked,
It whispered.
And yet—
There were glimpses,
brief flashes of fire in the trees,
the fall colors breaking through,
Burning against the grey curtain.
It was beautiful,
And it was haunting.
Enchanting,
Yet eerie.
The kind of morning

That holds you still,
That makes you wonder—
What lies beyond?
What waits in the hush?
Soon the season would be in full flame,
Autumn unfurling its gold and crimson.
But here, in the fog—
It was only a promise,
A whisper of what was coming.
A lie,
and a truth,
Woven into mist.

18 INK

Ink ran out—
bled across the pages,
staining the pink marker,
bleeding like memory,
Like sorrow that refuses to stay in its lines.
So much to say,
Yet so little time.
The pen and the page—
meeting again,
That old, fragile dance.
Words circling thoughts,
Thoughts circling wounds.
An exchange.
A release.
A confession.
All of it laid bare
before wandering eyes,
gleaming into a soul
already heavy—
stones tied to a heart,
dragging it down,
Pulling it deeper.
And still the question hangs,
Like a whisper in the dark:

How do you breathe
with all that weight
Pressing you under?

19 CABIN FEVER

It was those mornings and times.
When cabin fever hadn't quite set in—
The cold had begun,
But it hadn't become unbearable yet.
There was still some mobility,
still a bit of movement in the limbs,
Still laughter that hadn't frozen in the air.
But soon the cold would set in deeper,
slowly, quietly,
seeping into one's bones
Until even thought moved slower than the sun.
And soon we would become stir-crazy,
As the cabin fever dulls the mind.
Oh, how the mind can twist and turn—
restless, unanchored,
Pacing invisible corridors.
Cabin fever lurks about,
just waiting to devour you,
creeping in through the cracks
Where the wind hums low and hollow.
Having cabin fever isn't just for those.
stuck in the cabins of ships
On long seafaring journeys.

No—it feeds on those stuck about,
locked up in their rooms,
their towns,
Their thoughts.
It settles over the days.
like frost upon the windowpane,
Blurring the world beyond reach.
And the longer you sit with it,
The more the mind starts to go—
circling itself,
chasing the same thought
Until it becomes a murmur,
then a hum,
Then nothing at all.
Everything becomes feverish—
And dream.
The hours melt into one another,
The line between night and day dissolves,
And what was once familiar
feels far away,
Almost imagined.
And in that dream,
You begin to wonder
If perhaps it was never the cold
That truly crept in—
but something far quieter, waiting,
Inside you all along.

20 THE CUSP

Fall had come and gone.
It was on the tail end,
The cusp for winter.
Soon it would all be covered in snow—
the fields, the rooftops,
The winding forest paths disappear beneath white.
The leaves were almost all gone,
Yet sound still clung through the night—
the whisper of branches,
The soft rustle of what remained.
But the trees should become bare soon,
their arms reaching upward,
Silhouettes against a pale sky.
The coat of many colors—gone,
scattered to the winds,
To form along the forest floor.
A carpet of fading reds and golds,
Now damp with frost and shadow.
Frost-covered mornings appeared,
the world waking in quiet silver light,
And the cold nipping at your fingertips.
Each breath was a cloud that drifted and vanished.

Deer grazing on that what's left of green
grass,
moving slowly, carefully, and silently,
searching through the bits and pieces
Of all that seems to lack color.
A dullness settles in—
Not sadness, but stillness.
It seeps into the air,
Into the corners of the day.
The earth grows quiet,
And the heart feels it too—
this hush,
This is waiting for winter to come.

21 WINTER

Fall came fast,
And soon it turned winter.
And winter brought cold chills,
red cheeks,
And the tip of your nose was kissed by the frost.
Oh, how marvelous winter can be—
with its snow angels,
and its fluffy powdered snow,
its twinkling lights and its quiet magic
That falls softly over the world.
There's a hush in the air,
A stillness that settles deep,
As though the earth itself is holding its breath.
The trees stand cloaked in white,
The sky glows pale and distant,
And every sound feels softened,
As if wrapped in wool.
Children's laughter rings out through the cold,
echoing across the hills,
And footprints trail behind them—
Little stories pressed into snow.

The windows glow golden with firelight,
The scent of pine and cocoa drifts through
the room,
And outside, flakes dance beneath
lamplight.
Like a thousand tiny stars.
Fall came fast,
And soon it turned winter—
And though the world is cold,
It shimmers with warmth,
alive with the promise of peace
That only winter can bring.

22 BEHIND THE WRITERS

Those behind the writers—
the silent ones,
The ones whose voices are not heard on the page,
And yet they are witnesses to it all.
They watch, painstakingly,
hands covered in their loved one's writing,
Offering words of encouragement.
Oh, how beautiful it is
to have one such as this—
a writer's supporter,
a writer's friend,
A writer's husband.
There are so many who inspire our books,
standing behind us in the shadows,
encouraging us,
whispering words of faith,
offering quiet strength
To pick us up when we falter,
to remind us to keep going
When the page feels empty or heavy.
They speak to us,
They hear our stories and say,

"Yes," or *"No, what about this?"*
Their feedback, their presence—
resolute, unwavering—
our support,
our grounding,
Our quiet light.
And though they are not written into our stories,
They are there in every line,
In every moment of doubt overcome,
in every chapter completed,
In every word we dare to place on the page.
To those who stand behind us,
Who witnesses, who encourages,
Who believe even when we do not—
We write for you,
And we carry your strength with us always.

23 SILENCE

She has been screaming in the silence,
her voice so loud,
And her thoughts.
And yet she made quiet,
Not letting the words come out.
She observed and washed it all—
washed us,
Every lie tumbled about,
Each breaking point to an emerged.
And the way it caused a deeper and
deeper rift,
The way it seemed to become the bigger
tear,
And mending it only went so far,
For old wounds not let heal
It begins to fester.
It lingered in the corners,
a shadow moving through moments,
A weight pressing down unseen.
And still, she held it in,
watching, absorbing,
feeling every unraveling thread
Stretch tighter and tighter.
Until it ached beyond words.

The silence grew heavy around her,
And the world went on, unaware,
while inside,
The tumult swirled,
each unspoken word a stone
adding to the river
That threatened to drown her.
In memories she could not release,
In truth, she could not yet speak.
And in that quiet,
She became both witness and captive,
Feeling the fissures grow
Even as she tried
To hold the pieces together.
Old hurts are not allowed to heal,
only left to fester,
to carve the deeper and deeper rift
Those words, once freed, might one day
begin to mend.

24 WRITING

I felt stressed,
And felt like I wasn't really accomplishing anything,
But I spent all this time writing,
And it didn't seem to really go anywhere.
Until I actually sat down
to put it all together,
To start putting the bits and pieces where they belong,
to start filling out the books,
And seeing as the story is screwed together,
The bits and pieces stitched together,
forming a picture.
This writer thought a little too hard,
In this, one is a little too hard on oneself.
And yet, in the end,
You cannot rush a masterpiece.
You cannot force it.
It takes time.
Writing a book is no different.
It takes time,
And you're not going to get it right
the first couple of tries.
You're enough to shift things,

But you're going to have to edit
And try again.
And in those moments when it feels like nothing is moving,
When the pages pile up
And the story seems like a scattered mess,
Remember that this is part of the process.
Every line, every fragment, every thought
It is a step toward the whole.
A book is not built in a day.
It is built on hours of persistence,
in the slow gathering of ideas,
in the patient stitching of words
Until they form the picture, only you can see.
You will stumble.
You will doubt.
You will wonder if all this effort is for nothing.
And still, you keep writing,
Because the story demands it,
Because you cannot not tell it.
So, you edit,
You shift,
You try again,
And again.
And in the end, when the pieces finally

settle,
When the bits and pieces form something whole,
You realize that every moment of stress,
every doubt,
every little struggle
Was part of the masterpiece taking shape.
And that, perhaps, is the real reward:
not perfection, not speed, not ease,
But the slow, deliberate creation of
something only you could make.

25 FADING DARKNESS

She watched as the darkness slowly crept
away,
As the morning rays of the sun started to
rise,
And color started to spread and seep.
Into the world about.
Good morning, colors—
arising along the prairie,
Along the metal Alberta stretch.
The highway still glowed with headlights,
in the night sky, fading ever so slowly,
The morning arrived.
It was the quiet hour,
When night releases its hold,
And the world wakes in soft gold and pale
blue. Mist hung low over the fields,
and the hum of distant engines
Seemed almost to echo through time.
She breathed in the chill air,
watched the horizon catch fire,
and for a moment,
It felt as though the world itself.
was taking its first breath—
And she, too, was waking with it.

26 CABIN

Over the hill and around the bend,
Then there it is—Popular Street.
It was a beacon, calling out,
just as the first glimpse over that rise of the lake
Brings such a rush of joy.
I watched the colors change,
And the sun began to set.
The colors reflecting off the lake,
this cabin from my childhood,
All wrapped up in memories of this magical place.
The air smelled faintly of pine and earth,
and the gentle lapping of water against the shore
carried me back to summers long ago,
to days of endless light
And nights filled with stars.
I wonder if my future children.
would spend time here,
And what the future would bring.
Would they run along the paths I once knew?
Would they climb the hills and watch the

lake?
glitter in the sun,
Feeling the same rush of joy I once did?
And in that thought,
The place became larger,
stretching across generations,
holding the past, the present, and the
future
All together in its quiet, magical way.
This cabin, this lake, this hill, and bend—
They were more than just places;
They were memory and hope,
A story waiting to be told again and again.

27 HIDDEN

What stories are hidden within the forest
of popular trees?
What secrets do these tall trees keep?
What legends of old are waiting to escape?
She was awoken,
Surrounded by popular trees.
The wind moved the leaves every which
way—
It was as though they were all talking to
each other,
Telling each other secrets.
She listened closely,
Wondering if she could understand.
The rustle above sounded like whispers,
Soft and urgent, weaving through the
branches.
Sunlight danced through the canopy,
catching on the leaves,
Casting patterns that shifted and flickered,
Like messages written just for her.
Every tree seemed alive,
each one holding memories of countless
seasons,
of storms weathered and birds nested,

Of footsteps that had come and gone long before.
And in that forest,
surrounded by whispers and wind,
She felt as though the world had paused,
waiting for her to hear the stories
That had been hidden.
For longer than she could imagine.

28 FLICKERING CANDLES

Here she sat,
writing under the light
Of flickering candles.
It felt cozy,
Comforting in its own way.
The power had gone out—
Not something that happened often.
The time for candlelit evenings,
for rooms filled with candlesticks,
seemed far away,
A world almost forgotten.
Yet she couldn't help but wonder.
What it would have been like
to write before electricity,
When night itself was a companion,
and silence
It was not a burden but a gift.
Without all the modern-day distractions,
without the endless hum of screens,
the constant call of social media,
One could slip further inward,
closer to the quiet
Of one's own thoughts.
And in that stillness,

Words glowed brighter
Than the flame.

29 FROSTY DAYS

Oh, the whispers of winter—
That which goes wrestling in frost-covered trees,
the sounds,
The way everything crunches below one's feet,
The way one's fingers and toes can go numb from the cold.
Cold can slip its way into your bones,
Get under your skin,
and in those moments,
One finds oneself wrapped in the stillness of a winter night.
It's the kind of quiet that hums softly through the air,
That makes one long for a cup of coffee,
for warmth in the hands,
For the comfort of something familiar.
Oh, the marvels of winter—
cold days and colder nights,
The way breath turns to mist,
The way stars seem brighter against the frozen sky.
There is beauty in the chill,
In the silence that follows each snowfall,

In a world that glitters as though dusted with dreams.

30 SKY AWAKENS

In the wee early morning hours,
When the world was still dark before the sky awakens,
There were the lights of the town
reflecting across the water—
tiny ripples catching the glow,
Stretching out like threads of gold.
As she crossed upon the bridge,
The air hung heavy with mist,
and the hum of the river below
sounded almost like a heartbeat,
Steady and low beneath the stillness of dawn.
There it was—
the tiny little River valley,
The one that everyone said was so beautiful.
And they were right.
Even in the dark,
It was captivating—
the faint outlines of rooftops and trees,
the water glistening with borrowed light,
The whole valley was wrapped in quiet wonder.

For a moment, she paused there,
caught between night and day,
as the first pale streaks of morning
Began to stir the sky.
And in that hush before awakening,
She felt something—
a calm, a remembering,
as though the river itself
Was whispering, *Welcome home.*

31 MADNESS

It was confusing how the cabin fever had
begun before winter had even started—
As if the chill had crept in through the mind
long before the frost touched the ground.
It laid roots deep inside, invisible at first,
then winding through every quiet hour,
climbing, scratching, drawing in deeper,
Until the heart itself began to hum with the
strange tune of madness.
The thoughts tangled and knotted like
wild vines in a forgotten garden,
And no matter how I tried to prune them
back,
They grew stronger, curling around each
half-finished idea and memory.
I told myself it was only the weather,
only the coming dark pressing close against
the windows,
But the circles grew tighter,
round and round, like a fox chasing a hound
And a hound chasing a fox.
We don't all get to become friends with
the fox or the hound.
Sometimes, we only hear their howls

echoing through the trees,
a reminder of our own divided selves —
The wild part that runs and the weary part that hunts.
And so the days blurred.
The wind pressed its cold hand against the panes,
And I found myself listening to the silence.
As though it might offer an answer.
The kettle whistled like a small mercy,
Steam curling up like a thought that might escape the tangle.
Even in the stillness, something restless stirred —
a hunger for spring, for motion, for a clearing in the woods
Where the fox might stop running
And the hound might finally rest.
Until then, I remain here —
a little mad, a little alive,
trapped between the whisper of the trees
And the long echo of winter.

32 WINTER

Winter is a strange time.
It can cause one to get lost in the blizzard or snowed in,
One can feel trapped or cooped up in one zone,
And cold can slip into one's bones —
Slowly, quietly, until even thoughts begin to shiver.
It's the beginning of being cooped up,
of feeling restless and trapped,
The world is shrinking to four walls and a windowpane frosted over with sighs.
The cold is all around —
It hums in the walls,
It lingers in the air,
It creeps through the seams of doors.
And curls itself around the ankles like an unwelcome cat.
Stir-crazy, one begins to pace,
to count the cracks in the ceiling,
to watch the snow pile higher and higher,
As if it might someday seal the house in entirely.
And so it begins —
the slow unraveling of the mind,

The longing for sunlight, for green things,
for sound.
Cabin fever sets in,
not all at once but in small, quiet ways —
a sigh too long,
a silence too deep,
A thought that circles back again and again
like a bird at a frozen window.
Winter, in all its beauty,
It can be both a comfort and a cage.

33 THE COLDS RYTHEM

The cold nips, and it lingers, sticking its teeth into one's joints and knowing bones; it turns skin pink, and if cold, let loose, can go black and blue. The cold leaves bones and bruises all of its own.

There is a rhythm to the seasons, a call filled up in the wind. It brings messages carrying secrets and sends shivers down one's spine. The wind hums like an old song — one that's half-remembered, half-felt — and in its breath, it whispers stories of places long forgotten. The trees creak in answer, their limbs bowing under frost, and even the earth seems to listen, still and patient beneath its blanket of snow.

The cold is both cruel and kind — cruel in its bite, kind in its stillness. It quiets the noise of the world, softens the rough edges, and brings a hush to everything it touches. Yet beneath that hush, there's a pulse — faint but steady — the heartbeat of the land waiting for spring's thaw.

One learns to live with it, to find beauty in the bite and rhythm in the silence. For even in the coldest nights, when the air burns and breath turns to smoke, there's something alive in the stillness — something ancient and whispering, reminding us that every frost must eventually melt, and every silence carries the promise of a new beginning.

34 ECHOES OF THE NIGHT

Echoes of the night linger softly,
The air is still heavy with stars.
There they were —
faint lights clinging to the dark
As the sun began to rise,
its colors sweeping,
bleeding into shadow,
Painting the sky anew.
The night hums still,
echoing in the hush
Before morning breathes.
Stars dance,
hesitant to fade,
their shimmer folding
Into the warmth of day.
How beautiful —
this turning,
this gentle surrender
Where night becomes day,
And day becomes night again.
The echoes remain —
a whisper in the wind,
a trace of light on water,
the touch of God's fingerprints,

a work of art
spun between darkness
And dawn.

35 CIRCLES OF WINTER

Darkness had not fully set in —
The sun was still fading,
light still lingering,
a fragile thread of gold
Pulled thin across the horizon.
And yet, there was the moon —
rising, full and bright,
beautiful and radiant,
The sky welcomed her home.
She shone above the winding roads,
a guide for travelers,
A companion for the lost.
The roads were unpredictable,
Like the weather this time of year.
Winter wasn't endearing —
It was enduring,
pressing its way in,
just under the surface,
Waiting to take hold.
Fall and winter,
the cold months,
We're always harder.
One's body ached more,
The flare-ups came

Without warning.
It all seemed to go in circles —
layers of pain,
days of pushing through,
the quiet strength
Of simply continuing.
And beneath it all,
The moon still glowed,
a reminder
That even when warmth feels distant,
light endures —
soft, steady,
And impossibly brave.

36 CABIN DREAMS

Something about cabin fever —
being cooped up,
walls closing in,
Thoughts circling like winter winds.
Others think of cabin fever.
And dream instead
Of building a cabin.
That fever dream of making something
from one's own hands —
a log cabin rising from the ground,
investing time and energy,
learning how to save your timbers,
how to shave them,
how to measure them,
How to block them and change them,
How to line them up just right.
Slowly putting it together.
like a giant Lincoln log house,
then deconstructing it,
Moving it to its set location,
rebuilding again —
filling in all the pieces,
sanding and smoothing,
staining and building

this beautiful cabin,
A cabin in the woods.
It's not a challenge.
For the faint of heart, oh no.
This is a dream that takes time and energy,
A dream some will hold all their lives.
And never do.
And yet, a few —
brave, determined souls —
Set out to achieve it,
To build their cabin in the woods.
And there it stands,
beautiful as can be,
enchanting, warm, and cozy —
a home,
a retreat for all months,
not just the winter months,
Cozy as can be.
I watched it slowly come together,
this sort of Lincoln log house,
this puzzle of wood
Cut by hand —
timbers from one's own yard,
timbers of giant trees
They saw history in their lifetime.
All the stories within those limbs,
within those logs —

All the stories they keep.
What secrets do they whisper to the builder?
What have they witnessed?
Over the long years?
A builder constructs and builds —
blood, sweat, and tears,
sanding, slinging, chinking,
placing, and fitting it all,
until finally,
A cabin stands —
A dream made solid,
A fever made real.

ABOUT THE AUTHOR

Ruby F. Nazaruk lives in rural Alberta with her husband. A lifelong storyteller, she has spent her days surrounded by words — writing, reading, and sharing the stories that shape the heart of everyday life. From a young age, Ruby found magic in books and the power of imagination, a spark that continues to guide her creative journey.

She writes with the hope that her stories will inspire others to dream boldly, to put pen to paper, and to follow the quiet callings of their own hearts.

www.ingramcontent.com/pod-product-compliance
Lightning Source LLC
LaVergne TN
LVHW010941110826
845149LV00013B/2705

* 9 7 8 1 9 9 8 6 6 6 0 8 9 *